The Opposite Of Defeat

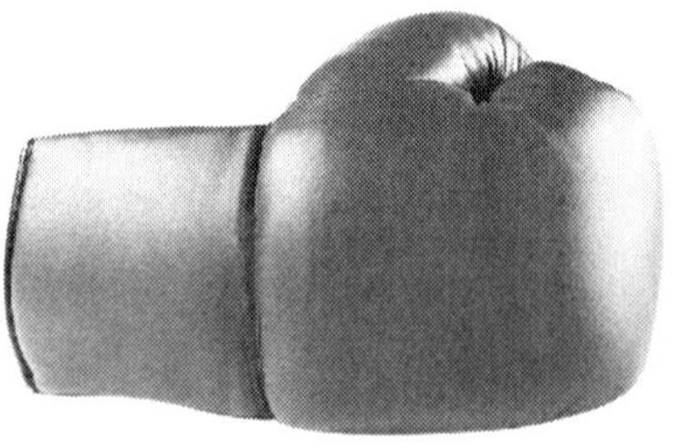

KEN EVANS
The Opposite Of Defeat

EYEWEAR AVIATOR

2016 SERIES

First published in 2016
by Eyewear Publishing Ltd
Suite 333, 19-21 Crawford Street
Marylebone, London W1H 1PJ
United Kingdom

Typeset with graphic design by Edwin Smet
Author photograph by Roger Morgan
Printed in England by Lightning Source
All rights reserved © 2016 Ken Evans

The right of Ken Evans to be identified as author of this work has been asserted in accordance with section 77 of the Copyright, Designs and Patents Act 1988

ISBN 978-1-911335-07-8

Eyewear wishes to thank Jonathan Wonham for his generous patronage of our press.

WWW.EYEWEARPUBLISHING.COM

> The lyric says there is a possibility for every sentient being to experience the opposite of the defeat we feel in our outer lives, although that opposite is not victory (defeat and victory being equally illusory) but transcendence of the idea of victory-defeat.
>
> John Burnside

Table of contents

- 9   Birthday Cake
- 10   Limestone Ghosts, Matlock Bath
- 11   Skins
- 12   The Chill of Meltwater
- 13   Consolations
- 14   Rebecca
- 15   The Kidney Consultant's Hairclip
- 16   Nil
- 17   I Remove Myself in Parts
- 18   Playing Dead
- 19   Taking A Slow Aim
- 20   Scissors
- 21   The Forest Edge
- 22   The Eyebrow Threader
- 23   The Wig-Keeper's Storeroom
- 24   A Sniff in the Art Gallery
- 25   Two People: The Lonely Ones
- 26   A Pair of Disappearing Heels
- 28   Down Dag's Lane
- 29   Iconoclast
- 30   These Things, for Definite
- 31   The Passions of Sleep
- 32   The Trapesius

- 35   Notes, Acknowledgements and Thanks

for Sheila, George and Harry

with love

Birthday Cake

Alone is a best guess, the time not auspicious or well-chosen.
Assume nothing about a bed.

It might be dawn, someone else's day, pre-claimed.

A tree in a northerly scratching at a window is not a narrative
it necessarily recognises, the moon is not clear, nor crescent-shaped.

It could be quiet to the point of shut-off, at home,
double-glazed with pale faces, a chink of familial tea-cups.

It can find me across the flotsam of drugs that keep me awake,
in time, or to rhythm, or even half sat-up:

an uncancelled standing order, a Web-bought thing I mean to send back –
it catches me here, now, in the middle of stuff,

rarely in the middle of a longed-for kiss or sunny beer garden,
winning a race on an unfavoured horse

or surprised by cake on my birthday, freckled knees:
sand-flies warming on the canvas of a fly-sheet,

a tent-zip stuck like a feather in gorse,
the beach widening in the imagination.

Limestone Ghosts, Matlock Bath

Miners long ago left their songs here
to birds, their ghosts to insurrectionary
bats, who call out their names.

Water down a wall like a miner's cap,
removed to wipe a brow, dropped
through the bird-throat of the dark.

I hear a pick-axe work, the rhythm of two
sorts of time: the human and a longer run,
chimed, then jarring notes, oppositional.

Nothing here, except the ghost of dreams,
a rocky clamminess for lichen to eke
a thin life from under background light.

One colour only escapes the cave mouth:
a miner, white-eyed with tiredness,
headed home, boots ringing on the limestone.

Skins

Overexposed prints in yellow,
empty boxes of festive cigars,
his medals, the cap he'd walk
the dog in, drifts of clothes,

his imprint on the bed
where we dress him
for the drive to hospital;
all this, easy to take.

The slippers are something
else. In their scuff and scurf,
most like him; side-elastic
stretched for his chilblains,

crumbs collected from tea-tray
suppers, a hole in one toe
where a nail rubs, the tartan's
straight lines pulled

from true by the curve
of his ankle bone.
I lift to smell, a votary,
disappearing into talcum.

These skins, as difficult to touch
as mushrooms I don't know
the names of; the feel of his hand,
the tendrils running to that machine.

The Chill of Meltwater

Born from the salt lick of a cow's warm tongue,
my father emerges from his ice-jacket; a revelation,
hair first, dripping; it is why I don't take praise well;
the Norse myth of Buri, father of the gods and Borr,
his son, a submergence to leave me wondering.

He re-opens veins to me just once; shows neighbours,
dragged in for Christmas drinks (strangers, in effect),
photos of me on the snowy-top of Kilimanjaro. He is proud,
showing-off: 'Look,' he seems to imply, *'even vegetarians
climb mountains!'* I brush off the compliment.

We never mention it (he is gone in five years),
though he seems pleased with a breakthrough. Now I,
father to my own Creation myth, use my salt tears to stop
ice forming, though frost is easier to build layers up
against than meltwater, which trickles through raw fingers.

Consolations

Had I a black tie
each time someone said
at least at funerals,
each new vanishing
should be waved off
with a fresh knot.

At least, they say,
the quantifiers'
turbid sum,
she didn't suffer,
matching each beat
of her mother's heart.

My own heart's pulsing,
the day my daughter
fails to arrive on time,
or at all,
stillborn
on seven months,
at least, they said.

Rebecca

Behind the frosted window glass, our grey
shadows pace, say the same things
over and over. A mid-wife turns the door-knob,
spins our known world upside down. Her arms
cradle a white bundle that sucks in light.
Lime walls of the Family Room, swaddled bands
laid in my wife's arms, the easy acceptance
of weight that isn't there. I lean into this dread,
this wanting, a naming: Rebecca.

The lips are shocking, raspberry-red.
Blood we gave her. My wife can't lift to share
her with me. I take up her arms in mine,
hold the sepulchre light, no cry or wriggle,
kiss the forehead, remembering in religion
or magic, spells are broken sometimes.
The skin is ivory, tight, the frost blue-veins,
her ears the size of my finger-nail, sea-shells
I could blow into, if I had breath, if I could howl.

The Kidney Consultant's Hairclip

Her hair secured by a brown clip,
not a strand left behind. I notice every
blemish of pink, each mole on her skin.
I depend on her choice of perfume,
her discreet jewellery. I examine her eyes
for signs: no problems at home
with partners. Her children, blameless,
will yet have a say in this, her grip, her weft.
Let her display a cruelty of resolve,
an insolence of skills, the odds-calling eye
of a croupier; grant her a surfeit of conviction.
She mouths my history to her clinical assistant,
tiny white down on her throat vibrating
as she discounts the conditions I don't have:
lung, heart and liver functions. She knows
I'm eyeing her for a sign of omnipotence,
that I've found it below the left ear at the pulse
on her neck. Her lips serve notice we're
serious here: theatre. Her long nights
studying to make this perfect.

Nil

The surgeon raises the headboard so I may sign the paperwork:
biro ink won't flow for me, lying on a pillow.

A release-clause for my own body-part, twelve-point Times New Roman:
'to confirm, the donor understands there's no advantage, the value is nil.'

It goes against every sinew to admit myself to hospital well,
to be made unwell, to give myself away.

'The value to you, the donor, is nil.' A chill annunciation
on which I falter, spiralling voices rise to shrill, choral nothing:

'no advantage, no gain, the value, nil.' This protocol
of the condemned: it takes a carefree blindness or iron-will

to underestimate the extent you bleed, when fully conscious, complete,
uncut, you read your own rolling credits: 'no gain, no advantage, nil.'

I do this, despite a brain. In ink, in blood, I sign, my signature
runs away down the page, an allograph. The anaesthetist has no second

thoughts, her mantra deep, repeatable, 'The value to you, the donor, is nil.'
The surgeon's scalpel-line on my bared left-side, peeking

through my bib like a sly wink, in indelible marker, gouging the words:
'the value is nil.' Counting down from five, I go under, not making it to zero.

I Remove Myself in Parts

The heart, of course, is first.
Aground, engine still
running, sub-marine.

Thought is next, present only
as sea is present, after
the tide slips out.

Fingers follow, slide
the rim of the bath, nail
scratching on white enamel.

Legs and thighs, after,
a diver pedalling downhill
through a weight above.

Ears lose their frequency,
pulses from a cave,
untentacled bubbles.

Last to go is my eyes.
They have a mind of their own.

Playing Dead

When it's light till late, lie on your back in the meadow,
let the grass prick your skin, a cellar of soil chill
your spine, flowers filibuster round a hem of trouser.

Pretend you are dead. The lamp above burns on,
regardless. Forget children's games, see the sky
instead through dead men's eyes, a red absence.

Ignore the charm-world of mortgage, house and lawn,
the lonely hypnosis. Imagine, instead, death tickles the inside
of your blouse, a stag beetle clambers damp hairs

on your wrist, drinks sweat from the crevices
of your splayed fingers, the stillness of a resting pulse:
an early fox ignores the fallen curve of your tumulus:

the owl blinks at your shadow, swivels to more
salvageable meat. The faintest scuffle of small life
being lost, sways the evening grass.

If you stay still, how long before you are greened,
bound to the earth? The sun sheds skins,
golden strips declining to ochre, then purple,
a slow fade, slithering into the land.

Taking A Slow Aim

The rabbit in my garden:
a cinnamon ruff down the spine,
mica-black eyes, comedy ears, a minesweeper
chomping a waterline of green.

I draw a bead, my Colt .45 automatic,
a steel bridge toward him.

He nibbles, the impunity of a daisy,
shakes, those whiskers
seem at the end of my nose

a muzzle-velocity of a thousand feet a second;
laggardly, as bullets go, allowing the two-thirty
grain cartridge, flying subsonic, to wobble.

So I aim where the soft key signs of life
dangle: his rising rib-cage dissolves,
a patch of brown on samphire.
I lean into the trigger.

Scissors

A newborn hangs from her hind-legs,
a glister of afterbirth. Wound inside
the mother, the lamb needs a last tug
on an unfreed knot, half-in, half-out,
a trapeze artist hung mid-air between
womb and the carrion-ground; ravens
tear and snap at the loose-end,
a flying, falling flash of scissors.
The mother is fear, confusion, complaint.

Cornered by the dry-stone wall,
she makes a hopping motion, rear-legs
hobbled by the pink-and-blue polyp
beneath the dags. Beaks pinch the eyes
of her young, the pulp of livery tongue,
a tiny pulse rises on a spilled stomach,
blood airing on boulder and thistle.
Frenzied with appetite, the ravens gorge
till satiated, neat house-clearers.

The Forest Edge

My fire blows smoke
holes in a tide
of green as an elk
strides, stiff-legged
from meditation, through
my newly-pitched camp.
Even the woodpecker
is tying up business
for the evening.
I scrub a cooking-billy
which slips my fingers
and dinks rocks,
a coppering echo.
The elk nostrils the sound,
finds nothing untoward,
ambles on, a brown ruminant.
The forest discriminates
by its silence; a vapour-trail
drags a banner of dusk
across the sky advertising
nothing special:
I am on the edge of it.

The Eyebrow Threader

They come in for a date, anniversary,
wedding; for hen-night's it's mandatory;
nails, lash-tints, pedicure: the boss says
upselling is everything. They don't know
what they want, customers, half the time.
Last year fish ate dead bits off your feet, for fun.

It's simple: you take a reel of sewing cotton,
make a necklace of thread around the neck,
tie and lift back over; keep taut, form a circle,
then spread the air to create a rectangle;
twist several times with your hands spread
out in front of you, the thread now makes an 'X'.

Take the twisted letter, align it dead centre.
Move it gently against the eyebrow, side
to side like a dance on 'Strictly'. Go right
to left, or whatever's natural. Lasso.
Start at the middle, above the nose,
the unibrow: top to bottom, sidle.

The lower eyebrow is most sensitive.
Peachy hairs higher up are less painful
to the tug. I become that final gentleness
of the embalmer, my hands relaxing clients
for whatever comes next. The boss winks,
he thinks I'm good and I tell him, *Dead right*.

The Wig-Keeper's Storeroom

Egg-heads, softly cranial, settle to their necks
on shelves under strip-light, the pursed lips of
silent prophets awaiting re-birth, blind,
Oedipal, postiches of virgin Russian hair,
grown by girls on follicle diets, sold in swatches
to middle-men. Drawn through the hackle twice,
their ends evened for an equal fall, lustrous
curtains of concealment and reveal, a halo
for the person-to-be to shelter beneath,
wearer and wig, bonded by sweat and anxiety:
a prosthesis, both like and unlike, ourselves.

A Sniff in the Art Gallery

With the long face of a quiet shift,
Security is reflected in the glass doors

separating eras. Perspex panels share
the meaning of it all: a brown bird

in a window on a twig rises, the bob
of a branch warps the light a moment.

In a corner of the gallery, a sniff:
I drag myself from the artist in front

to check my periphery, but as I swivel,
the other visitor, missed once already,

seeps through white walls soundlessly,
a conjurors' sleight of hand, a deception,

mere shadow off the parquet, the tilt in tone,
tawny to ochre, so fast, when I look to check

what I saw, I really saw, the other,
the bird and twig, Security even, are gone.

Two People: The Lonely Ones
after Edvard Munch's, 'The Lonely Ones', (Woodcut, 1899) Whitworth Art Gallery, Manchester

The only man-made thing seen
from space is the distance
between a man and a woman:

no great wall, deep-sea trench,
as visible as their crater-edge;
no horizon, a flat perspective

held in tension by steel lines
only making their separateness
more tangible. A white dress,

she hovers, no more than a ghost to him,
shorn of understanding as the stone
that holds him: she is water, elliptical.

Sea and stone, mutual incomprehension,
backs to us, no faces, voyeurs
to their own dissolution.

His right arm bent, perhaps hand in pocket,
jangles keys in frustration, unable
to reach out from himself.

Her hand fingers a damp handkerchief,
we can't know for sure, anymore
than they do. The little they share is strife.

Slate-blue sea, unyielding stone: unable
to span the gap, they are unplinthed,
awaiting the tide.

A Pair of Disappearing Heels

By the kick of your legs,
our row is not over:
body green, each shoulder
whitening on the alternate rise,
fall, of your stroke; ears pressed
under the smooth prosthetic
of a swim-cap.

Your face dark glass,
eyes shut against me.
I could halt your
plough from the pool-side,
touch; still the stop-clock
of your anger, smooth
the furrows.

The fin of your hip,
your costume clinging
as you carve a shipping-lane,
lips set on the long lengths
of determination.
The fourth glass
of our argument, swallowing us:

a wash of words,
unstoppable: a tide we can't
take back, the framed-glass
mirror of our faces
hitting waves, spiked
blue geometries
splinter.

An arc of arms,
throwing punches of light,
eddying down lanes
at the deep-end. At two metres
twenty, your spin-turn, a shine
of heels disappearing,
your bottom, risen, waning.

Down Dag's Lane

This morning, down the snicket
by your house at the terminus
of our conversation, more
invigorated than in years,
buoyed by your willingness
to broach the difficult,
my tongue, the small frictions
of a leaf, grubbed between
my thumb and forefinger,
a burring; ridge after soft
green ridge serrating
to an horizon. I lick
my finger, taste the green
fact that mountains
can seem both for
and against us.

Iconoclast

Dread I have a premonition of death
and miss it;
Dread, in and out of fluency, I wake
in a new language;
Dread everything is freely available
only I skip the fact,
that night is now perpetual oil,
and I adjust my eyes to it;
there's a new carbolic of purity
I neglect to wash with.
Dread an appearance of vandalism
while I smash nothing of significance;
Dread love, as a vitamin-deficiency
of my rickety heart.
Dread, in our old age, we kick out
at each other from our gentle recliners.
Dread I ever lose the protein of urgency.

These Things, for Definite

Among the 12,000 lies I've forgotten,
11 things hold true; that 93% of birds vote
for dawn, the rest are unreachable; that the heart
pumps 4 times its own weight in 1 minute, keeps
perfect time for half a century; that most people
function only as strangers; that I only drink
for the hangover, a muting; that 11% of guide dogs
in New Zealand are short-sighted; that you can
buy insurance to cover cryogenically freezing
your head; that flies on a Welsh hill-farm live
the Dream, if only retrospectively; that U.S. toddlers
don't wish to murder their fathers; that owners
of car-stickers saying, *One Life, Live It*,
probably don't; that everything under Africa
is part of China; that drinking your own urine
is only ever a stop-gap.

The Passions of Sleep

She wears the light material of sleep,
a child in organza folds, over the woman's
fuller lips; hints there too, of an older self,
a passenger, early, to a waiting platform.
Her face articulates according to the dreams'
spring; light or comic; ironic and darker,
perplexed; angry now, or excited; a breezy
leat, flush with recollection. The turnover
on the bed, a white border of a photo needing
a title, recalled too long after to name the place.
The films of her past and future open, feeding
the eyes, spreads across her dimpled surface,
the twisted sheet, her kneaded pillow, milling
images, and in every version, she's running.

The Trapesius

The sun in the blind is a bird in a cat's mouth:
phone, glasses, wallet, I collect myself from the sofa,
then to your kitchen in search of coffee.

Your nightdress eddies round the door, a milk-space
between your pale shoulder straps, the spine and scapula.
As you stretch for a mug, your shoulder-blade is a boulder

smoothed by river water, shone through with light. I gaze
a second too long at this space in your back, unreachable,
I imagine, even by you.

Notes, Acknowledgements and Thanks

Special thanks to Todd Swift and Cate Myddleton-Evans for their editorial inputs and advice, improving the first draft of this pamphlet. Thanks to Edwin Smet for his fantastic cover design.

Acknowledgements are due to the Editors of the following publications where these poems, or earlier versions, first appeared: *The Lighthouse Literary Journal*; *Obsessed with Pipework*; *Envoi*; *The Interpreter's House*; *The Glasgow Review of Books*; *The Island Review*; *Manchester Anthology 2015*; and on the poetry websites – www.andotherpoems.com edited by Josephine Corcoran; www.clearpoetry.wordpress.com, edited by Ben Banyard, to whom gratitude and thanks.

'Birthday Cake' was commended in the Troubadour International Poetry Competition 2015. 'The Wig Keeper's Storeroom' won 2nd prize in The Poets & Players Competition 2016, (Judge: Jacky Kay).

'At Least' featured on the Poetry School's website in an earlier version of this work shortlisted in the Poetry School's 'Primers'/Nine Arches Press Competition for a debut collection (2015); also featured, along with other poems here, in the Bare Fiction Debut Collection shortlist judged by Andrew McMillan in 2015.

The John Burnside title and preface quote, 'The Opposite of Defeat' (Page 1) is taken from *Strong Words: Modern Poets on Modern Poetry*, ed. W.N Herbert & Matthew Hollis, (Bloodaxe Books, 2000).

A special debt of gratitude is owed to John McAuliffe, Co-Director of the Centre for New Writing, Manchester University, who read and critiqued many of these poems.

Thanks also to Emma Simon for her generous and thoughtful editing.

Also Karen Wheatcroft, Estelle Goodwin, Peter Viggers, Shirley Nicholson and fellow students on the Creative Writing Master's at Manchester (2014-15), who commented on many of these poems.

EYEWEAR AVIATOR

2016 SERIES

CLAIRE WILLIAMSON
Split Ends

ELIZABETH PARKER
Antinopolis

PAUL DEATON
Black Knight

GEOFF GILBERT & ALEX HOUEN
Hold! West

MICHAEL CONLEY
More Weight

CAL FREEMAN
Heard Among The Windbreak

KIMBERLY CAMPANELLO
Hymn to Kālī

LINDSEY HOLLAND
The Lanterns

JAMES FLYNN
Arriving At The Capital

KEN EVANS
The Opposite Of Defeat

More to come...

WWW.EYEWEARPUBLISHING.COM